You're Everything You've Ever Needed

A POETRY COLLECTION

You're Everything You've Ever Needed

You're everything you've ever needed
Copyright © 2024

All rights reserved

No part of this book may be reproduced, distributed, or transmitted in any form or by any means, including electronic, mechanical, photocopying, recording, or otherwise, without the author's prior written consent.

Disclaimer:
This book contains explicit, mature content and language.

Formatting, poems and cover by Madison

ISBN: 978-1-7382816-0-2

Madison Farraway
Ontario, Canada

Maddocuments.contact@gmail.com
www.maddocuments.com

You're Everything You've Ever Needed

To heal • To reclaim • To Grow

You're Everything You've Ever Needed

contents

reclaiming..............................7

rebuilding............................41

healing.................................97

growing..............................155

You're Everything You've Ever Needed

this is a journey of self-love,
self-discovery, healing and a reminder;
that you're everything you've ever needed
all along.

You're Everything You've Ever Needed

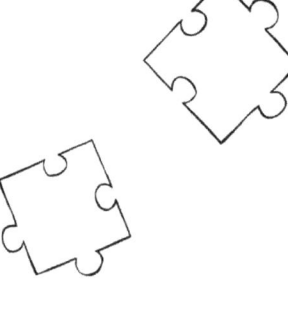

chapter one
reclaiming

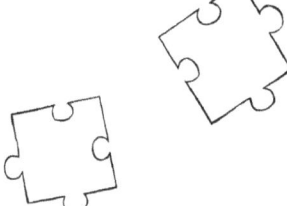

You're Everything You've Ever Needed

our conversations were so intensely intoxicating that it was addictive; i compromised myself *to be loved.* i compromised myself and my well-being to *feel* loved. the first time someone held me, kissed me, and then told me they loved me, i felt every emotion i could've in those moments.
to think of someone so deeply and intensely that you feel you are whole;
to love someone so much
you don't care if they love you back.

i know what it is like to love someone that isn't good for you and to feel it in every inch of your skin. to then leave them–felt like my brain, heart, and soul had been ripped out–every sense of self withering away with them too.
but in a painfully beautiful way,
that was fulfilling, too.
i felt in that moment so fucking empty; it was almost fulfilling to feel nothing for once, after all.

- *codependent*

a one-sided relationship

when you try to sustain a relationship alone,
you will grow tired, exhausted, and empty.
because it is impossible,
a relationship takes two.
trying to sustain a relationship alone is like being in the middle of the ocean, and you've been treading water for far longer than you should've.
you will fade into an emotionless being, until the rest of you is a ghost of a soul you once were.

do not drain yourself because someone cannot give you the same amount of love you put in.
you deserve to be loved whole, not half.
you shouldn't feel like your emotional needs are, or have been neglected, and you shouldn't feel lonely in their presence, you shouldn't have to tolerate disrespectful behavior, or try to convince yourself this is healthy and normal, it's not.–you do not neglect them, so why do you neglect yourself?

You're Everything You've Ever Needed

do not continue to stay when you know you should leave.

and do not continue to hurt yourself by loving someone who doesn't reciprocate the same effort you put in.

being alone and being lonely

the tension grows, and the emotional need to be needed fades with every exhale.
every sigh and every shrug fueling this feeling of uncertainty but draining every feeling you have ever felt till you are an emotionless being of the person you once were together until you are left with a hole in your heart where that void grows.
you shouldn't be with someone who makes you crave being alone physically,
because being with them makes you feel empty and unhappy.

you should be with someone
who makes hours feel like minutes,
someone who knows what makes your soul light up.
most importantly, you should be with someone who fills you, not drains you like you are their favorite drink leaving you empty and dry of the person you were.

the person who is breaking you will not fix you

an addictive cycle-

You're Everything You've Ever Needed

the highs put you on top of the world,
and the lows are low,
really fucking low.
but that is what makes the good times seem so
good.

somehow, you may find yourself holding onto
something, onto someone,
because that relationship is your drug; remember
the person who is breaking you will not fix you.
i hope you heal and free yourself from any
resentment for staying when you know you
should leave. it is not too late;
you do not have to wait for an excuse to leave.
i plead that you find the strength
to pull yourself out of this hole.

You're Everything You've Ever Needed

if they walked out on you

when they walked out on you,
it hurt and i know you feel like the whole world just came crashing down,
but they did you a favor;
they left someone they didn't deserve and set you free of the hope that they would be better.
you didn't lose them; they lost someone who loved them more than they deserved.
so, don't think you have lost them,
but instead were set free of a love you didn't need,
a love that you were left with the short end of the stick when you should have had it all.

You're Everything You've Ever Needed

there laid a storm within their eyes,
hate and anger in their heart,
and disgust upon their skin.
i watched them scratch and scratch,
until nothing remained.
as the realization it was not their fault grew,
they flowered into something like never before.

it wasn't your fault. i'm sorry you have had to carry this burden alone. i promise you will heal, grow, and come out of this.

You're Everything You've Ever Needed

there is more for you outside of these walls, there is more love out there for you.

You're Everything You've Ever Needed

do not disregard how they told you they loved you
and then showed you they didn't.
a person who loves you wouldn't do that to you.
do not disregard the constant lows
to allow the temporary highs to keep you with
someone unworthy of you and your love.
wanting to be here with them
 is not a reason to stay; it is not a reason to keep
allowing yourself to be hurt.
someone is out there waiting
to give you all the love you deserve.
those temporary waves of happiness
are not worth a lifetime of lows.

- *there is more for you outside of these very walls*

reminder: you are not hard to love. someone who makes you feel that you are does not love you.

someone who does not appreciate you just for your presence alone does not value you.

You're Everything You've Ever Needed

do not change yourself,
your values, or your morals
to fit into another person's life.
another person's perception of perfection.

- *the right person will love you as you are,
for who you are*

You're Everything You've Ever Needed

you compromise yourself
to make them happy, and to be loved.
little pieces of you beginning to drift away,
fragments of you falling apart until you are nothing
but a ghost of a soul you once were.

do not alter yourself, do not change your dreams,
desires, or boundaries to fit into another's life.
do not lose yourself to gain them or mold yourself
to fit into someone else's life other than your own.

You're Everything You've Ever Needed

you can miss who they once were
and hate who they have become.
do not let this keep you where you are.
do not let the thought that they will come back and
be the person you need them to keep you here,
and keep you in an overwhelming sense of
uncertainty.

You're Everything You've Ever Needed

those apologies and those promises you hold onto
are empty, i know you're trying to find all the
reasons they are not, but they are.
every time they hurt you, fresh promises are
brought to your attention.
the love that has been lost for months is back,
and the effort seems to have been made until you
are right back where you started.
this behavior is no longer a one-time mistake but a
choice or habit.
this is manipulation, as they tell you everything you
sincerely want and need to hear, but
they do not intend to change their actions
and they will continue manipulating you.

you do not deserve to put yourself through something you have already lived.

You're Everything You've Ever Needed

the unresolved trauma from your childhood will
follow you throughout adulthood and
you may search for that trauma within a place,
person, or thing.
it is not good, but that may be all you know.
sometimes, we find comfort in what has hurt us and
will continue to because it is familiar.
healing from that initial trauma is realizing that it
wasn't your fault and you didn't deserve that.

You're Everything You've Ever Needed

you will find clarity when you realize
and accept that maybe,
just maybe leaving could provide you with more
peace then staying in that toxic relationship,
or the environments you surround yourself with.
that maybe it is easier to remove yourself from the
toxicity than trying to make something work that
isn't ever going to.

You're Everything You've Ever Needed

the toxic relationships that you may have in your
life, the relationships that you constantly find
yourself running back to.
no matter how low they can make you feel at times,
because the temporary highs
seem to make the lows manageable.

those toxic relationships are similar to addictions,
a drug that you know is harmful to you.
still, you find yourself returning for more.
but the longer you stay,
the more destructive they become.
the longer you wait, the harder it is to leave.
please know that you cannot heal while you are
surrounded by the very thing that keeps hurting you.

You're Everything You've Ever Needed

you would have loved them forever.
you would have stayed forever if it were up to you,
but you lost yourself in the process–you lost the
parts of you that were fluent in boundaries– trying
to find the person they once were, the soft, gentle
person they were, until they weren't.

- *loving a narcissist*

You're Everything You've Ever Needed

you resent the world,
and your eyes have flames of rage and anger.
you hold on to the hope that one day,
you will wake up from this daydream,
and they will return to you.
when you resent the world for continuing to live without them, you are abandoning the most healed parts of you by not accepting what cannot be changed. don't resent yourself for existing without them. you deserve to be free and happy, but know you will meet again.

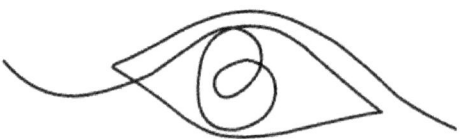

*don't try to convince yourself
that someone
is something they are not.*

You're Everything You've Ever Needed

they never loved you,
and you know that deep down.
you put your head underwater to quiet all the noises,
all the voices that remain above water–
the ones you can never seem to get away from.
–you know it would never work.
so you submerged yourself underwater, right?
when you met them, you knew it wouldn't work;
you put your head underwater,
hoping that it would be different this time when you
came up for air.
you liked them and expected your head and heart to
align one day, but they never did.
they never loved you, and they made it clear.
why do you keep trying to convince yourself
otherwise?

You're Everything You've Ever Needed

you spend more time in bed listening to the songs
that remind you of most of them than anything else;
they consume most of your days and most of your
nights.
i see the beauty in that–you're so in love with them
that they have become a part of you, and now that
they are gone, you feel lost without them.
that's why you spend most of your days in your bed,
locked in your room, thinking of them, wondering if
they could have been better, and maybe you'd be
better, too; the cycle remains the same.

you base your entire self-worth in the hands of
someone else, and now you feel lost without them.
in this state, you must change the cycle of thoughts
that go round and round every day and every night.
you must do what is good for you and let them go.
you cannot keep hurting yourself by holding onto
them when you need to let go.

adolescent love,

how do you love someone
without giving yourself up?
how do you trust them without letting all your walls
down and essentially giving them a handbook on
how to hurt you. they can rip you apart so quickly
and easily; then any love you have ever felt for
yourself leaves with them, too.

adolescent love,
how do you love someone without basing your
whole self-worth in their hands?

You're Everything You've Ever Needed

art will not fill this void,
lust will not sever the darkness
that lives embedded deep within.
being wrapped up in a soul and intertwined in their
mind is not enough to fill this hole.
because being attached to the hunger
of repetitive lust means more,
and painfully holding onto the hope that one day,
just maybe, the skin that lives above these bones
will feel like home.

- *lust will not fill the void*
  that lives dormant deep within

You're Everything You've Ever Needed

she sat empty-handed at the end of her bed,
she had been there all day,
because of the pain you left her with.
and even knowing you are the person who caused
the pain, it's still you who she wants to comfort her,
hold her, and love her.

- *the irony of pain is wanting to be comforted by the person who caused the hurt*

a game of chasing love,
with someone who is never
going to stop running.

You're Everything You've Ever Needed

it is heartbreaking to love someone who doesn't
love you back or love you in the ways you need
them to love you.
it's painful to chase love,
a love that doesn't plan on ever being caught.
this romanticized love, or lust,
where that chase is thrilling.
watching someone fight to get what they want
while running, never letting them get too close
but making them think they might.
run from this kind of love,
a 20th-century type of love.

- *a 20th-century kind of love*

maybe in the next lifetime,
they loved you
the way you needed to be loved.

You're Everything You've Ever Needed

maybe in the next lifetime, they will be the person
you needed them to be,
because at one point in between now and then, they
were that person.

maybe in the next lifetime
they will give you everything you want,
everything you needed,
everything they promised.

You're Everything You've Ever Needed

the lack of love they fail to give you,
has nothing to do with you.
it is not that you are not smart enough,
funny enough, or the love
you share is not enough. you are enough,
you are just looking in the wrong direction.
their lack of love has nothing to do with you,
it has everything to do with them.
do not question your worth, or shave pieces of
yourself off to be less for them.
do not question every piece of yourself in exchange
for an ounce of their love,
the right person will love you for you.

- *the cost of false love*

You're Everything You've Ever Needed

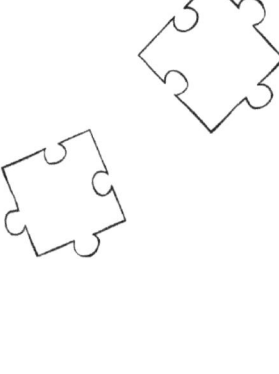

chapter two
rebuilding

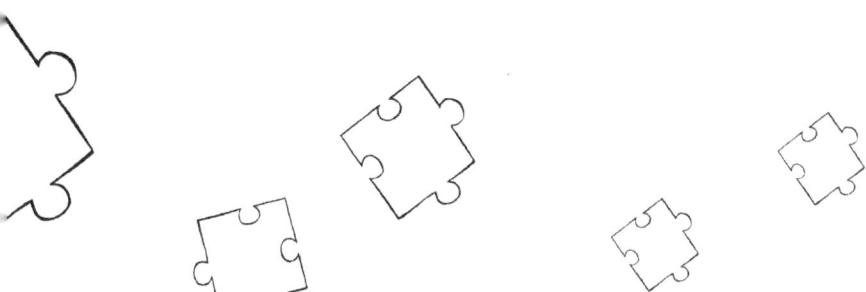

sometimes,

the people we want most

are the people we are best without.

You're Everything You've Ever Needed

there is a reason why our hearts connect more to
certain people and less to others.
the worst part is that sometimes those are the people
we don't get to keep forever.
sometimes, the people we want most are the people
we are best without.
people will come into your life to teach you,
to love you, and to show that you are worthy of
more. however, sometimes we don't get to keep the
people we want most–their memories, lessons, and
love–is what will remain embedded within.

change can be scary,
so take baby steps.
remember change is critical
for personal growth and to evolve.

You're Everything You've Ever Needed

growth can be uncomfortable,
and change can be, too.
we do not know what lies ahead of us, but we
should not let the fear of the unknown keep us here.
take baby steps,
set goals and work towards them.
healing relies on you and only you.
you can have help,
but when the sun begins to set
and the day turns to night,
it is you, and only you, who decides to make the
change for yourself.

You're Everything You've Ever Needed

you deserve
to be loved unconditionally,
do not let anyone make you
believe you are worth less than
that.

You're Everything You've Ever Needed

i hope you believe you deserve the love
you give to others.
i hope you believe you deserve to be listened to
when you need to talk
and be comforted when you need it most.
but most of all,
to be loved in the same ways you love them.

- *to be loved unconditionally*

you were perfect before it all

the trauma you endured wasn't necessary.
you didn't deserve those events.
you were perfect before it all.
maybe it carved and molded you to be a better person, but it didn't need to happen because that implies that you would've been unable to improve and grow without it.
trauma changes us,
the way we think, and the way we feel.
so maybe it changed you; perhaps now you have a different perspective on life,
for the better, or maybe for the worse.
but it didn't need to happen,
because you were perfect before it all.

remind yourself that
grieving is apart of the process,
and it is okay to hurt.

You're Everything You've Ever Needed

when you detach yourself from the identity of that
initial feeling,
of that initial love,
you will grieve.

to love and yearn for someone or
for something is painfully beautiful.
you are letting go,
but you are not just letting go of them.
rather, a piece of yourself, too.

- *remember that the feeling
  of grief will not last forever*

You're Everything You've Ever Needed

when you detach yourself and begin to put yourself
first, you do not have to beg them to stay.
you do not have to hold onto that hope
that they will be the person you need them to be.
you will not have to carry the weight of their
toxicity anymore; you do not have to convince your
friends that they are someone they are not.
when you let go of them,
you will see that you deserve so much more, so
much better.

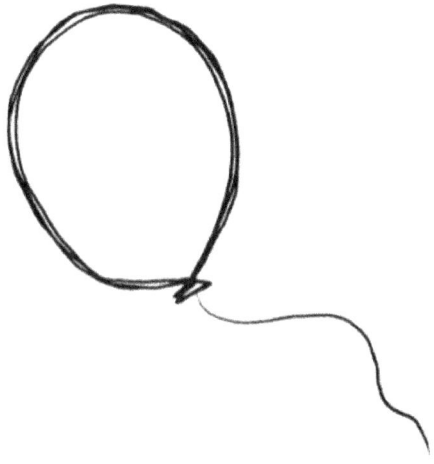

You're Everything You've Ever Needed

you doubt yourself until you do it.
you realize it was all just in your head.
it is scary to do something when the outcome is unknown, but once you do it
you realize that it wasn't as bad as you imagined it, and maybe you would have regretted it if you hadn't.

- *the same goes when you are moving on from those toxic relationships in your life.*

be selfish when it comes to your needs, and do not feel sorry because you care and love yourself.

how can you be there for others if you are not there for yourself first?

You're Everything You've Ever Needed

release yourself from the guilt you hold onto,
it is okay if you need to step back from the people
you care most about to focus on your well-being.
it is okay to ask for help,
and to reach out,
but most importantly, put yourself first.

this is your life,
do not feel guilty for taking the time to find your
way back to yourself.
it is not selfish; it does not imply you are a failure or
a bad person.
you are doing what is best for you,
what may be best for the people around you too.

loving the right person

i know it may hurt,
i know you may be searching for them in every
person, every crowd, and every car that passes by,
hoping just one day you will see them.
that maybe one day they will see you
the way you need to be seen.
but think of it– if you can love a person who does
not see your value, or who does not see your worth,
if you can love the wrong person so intensely,
profoundly, and passionately–imagine how you
could love someone who loves you as deeply, and
as intensely as you love them, or even more.
if you can value the wrong person, imagine how
much love you could give to someone who values
you as much as you value them. someone to love
you in ways you deserve,
and in ways you didn't think were possible.

You're Everything You've Ever Needed

you found joy in being alone among that heartache and peace in being alone.
you managed to find comfort in soft, whispered silence; those whispers live deep within you and keep you awake while everyone is sound asleep.
you found relief in not having a sudden argument, you found yourself, and then you found peace.

You're Everything You've Ever Needed

you deserve to be loved wholeheartedly
every day,
every moment,
every second.

not every other day,
not every other week,
or every other month.
you deserve to be loved every day,
and every moment for the rest of your life.

do not leave yourself behind, you need to take care of yourself emotionally and physically too.

You're Everything You've Ever Needed

if you are the one everyone goes to vent,
please don't leave yourself behind.
i know you are the backbone and
it is amazing to be there when people need someone
to cry on or laugh with, but don't forget to be there
for yourself too; you are a caretaker for many
people, but do not neglect yourself, care for your
mind, body and soul as much as you do for them.

do not apologize because you felt the pain of their disrespect, lies, love, hate and selfishness. do not apologize because it feels almost as if they have taken anything good you've ever felt about yourself, and burned it.

- *do not apologize for feeling*

You're Everything You've Ever Needed

when you fear change,
you also fear self-improvement.

You're Everything You've Ever Needed

we are meant to outgrow certain people,
there are reasons why you outgrow places and
hobbies, too. change is okay, change is critical for
growth as humans. so don't be ashamed if you are or
have outgrown someone or something you thought
you would've loved for a lifetime.

pain is our greatest teacher,
pain teaches us
what we will tolerate,
and what we will not.

pain allows room for change,
use it to your advantage.

chaos is a narcissists comfort

they will thrive on the intensity
while burning a hole through your soul.
they will find their way to tear you down,
making you the villain of every story,
always making you feel like you're not good
enough. all while turning your admiration into
despair and self-confidence into self-doubt.

You're Everything You've Ever Needed

it is over,
as hard as that is to accept, you have to.
you cannot keep trying to fix something
meant to stay broken.
you cannot keep trying to force something together
that is made to remain apart.

You're Everything You've Ever Needed

love isn't supposed to hurt that much.
if you have longed to feel loved by the wrong
person, imagine how much love there would be
with the right person.

You're Everything You've Ever Needed

you did not choose this life or this pain you may be experiencing, but please do not take that pain or that hurt and turn yourself into something a year from now you wouldn't recognize. sometimes, the finest souls are the ones who have experienced the most tremendous amounts of pain. sometimes, the strongest people didn't choose to be strong.
if that seems to apply, please do not let this pain turn you cold, remain soft. do not change who you are, even when it feels like the world is crashing. hold onto hope, and dedication, remember you will heal.

- *pain is your greatest teacher.*

You're Everything You've Ever Needed

life is messy and complicated.
the chaos lives rent-free within and feeling peace
may feel like you are reaching for the stars.
let me tell you it will not feel like this forever.
take care of your well-being,
and do what is best for you.
after all this, you will find peace,
and everything else will fall into place.

- *i promise*

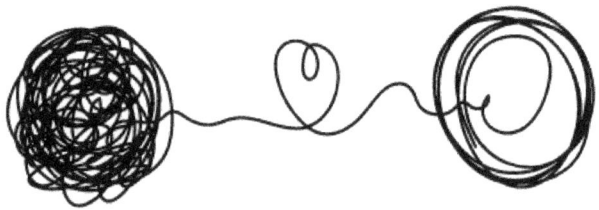

i believe things happen when they are supposed to happen.
timing is everything, and your time will come.

so don't feel you are lost or behind, you are putting all the pieces together day by day **even when you don't realize it.**

You're Everything You've Ever Needed

you feel like you have been dead-stopped in your tracks, and no longer have a purpose.
you do have a purpose–it is just yet to be revealed to you–take this as an opportunity to try new things, meet new people, and take the time to learn about yourself. who you are, what you want out of life, and who you want to become.
but let me tell you that you will end up where you belong soon enough,
so do not worry if you feel lost now.

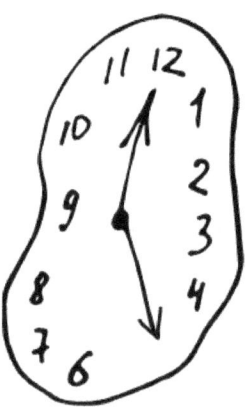

You're Everything You've Ever Needed

you are doing better than you realize,
it is brighter on the other side of this very tunnel.
it is okay if you feel exhausted,
it is okay if you are tired,
it does not make you weak to reach out and ask for
the help you may need, or the help you want.

You're Everything You've Ever Needed

remember that your pain is beautiful,
because you loved and yearned for something.
you are grieving,
and you know that means it was real.

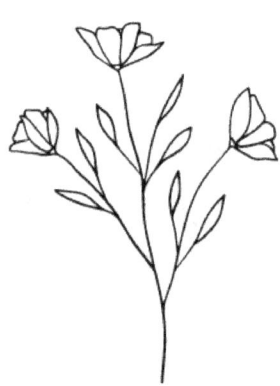

You're Everything You've Ever Needed

i hope you are proud of yourself.
i hope you are proud of all your accomplishments,
you did it. it does not matter if they are small or big
they are wins.
think about every sacrifice,
every obstacle you have suffered in your lifetime,
all that you have endured.
look at where you are now,
and how far you can go.

You're Everything You've Ever Needed

i believe things happen
the way they are supposed to happen.
there are reasons why some things end,
there is a reason why we detach ourselves
from certain people and places.
some things just happen as they are supposed to,
even when we don't expect or want that thing to
occur; sometimes there aren't answers, so don't
cause yourself pain by trying to find them all.

You're Everything You've Ever Needed

the right person will listen to you,
the right person will take the time
to get to know you.
the right person will know
everything that makes you laugh,
everything that makes you cry,
and most of all,
everything that lights up your eyes.

You're Everything You've Ever Needed

i see the sadness that lies beneath that smile,
i feel the hate that lies within your heart,
i know the anger in your soul.
you are stuck, and you're getting tired.
this will come to an end soon enough,
just wait and see how much brighter it gets.

seasonal depression

it is september,
and you can smell the falling leaves through the air,
they remind you of a time last year.
please remind yourself you have been here and you
made it through.
please do not spend time giving this more fear.
you will be okay.
you've been here before,
and you will get out of here.

think of yourself and how you want to be treated and respected.

what you allow into your life, and surround yourself around is what you will get,
it is a reflection of one's self.

You're Everything You've Ever Needed

you have to put your boundaries first
before your empathy.
may your heart and head not be aligned, but it is
crucial because if not,
you will always make sense of how they treat you.
your heart will always justify how they hurt you.
you cannot allow yourself to get walked over
constantly; it isn't fair to you or them.

You're Everything You've Ever Needed

love makes us believe in people
we know won't change,
and see past all the problems and toxicity.
so we hold onto those people, hoping that one day
they will be the person we need them to be,
that one day they will see the hurt they are causing.

You're Everything You've Ever Needed

you love them,
you care for them, and that is beautiful.
but remember it is not your responsibility to try to
fix someone; more importantly, try to help someone
who doesn't want help nor want to change.
you cannot save them from the habits they continue
to do. i know you love and care for them,
but you cannot break yourself trying to heal them.
you cannot lose yourself
trying to fix the habits they created.
love, support, and be there for them but if they don't
want to put in the effort to make the change for
themselves, you cannot force them.
i know you love and care for them,
but care for yourself too.
love yourself, too.

reminder:

you may feel a sense of guilt while healing, this is a sign of growth.

You're Everything You've Ever Needed

you may feel guilty when you are healing from all
the thoughts and memories within your soul.
when you feel guilt,
it is a sign you are healing and growing.
you are recovering from things you didn't even
know were living dormant.
this guilt you feel will pass
as you let go of all that has brought you pain,
all that has hurt you.
when you heal, you will no longer feel this.
as the guilt rises off your shoulders,
because you will realize you deserve to be happy
and you didn't deserve to be holding onto all that
hurt, all of that pain by yourself for all that time.

You're Everything You've Ever Needed

you are everything you have ever needed
to change the life ahead of you.
you have scars,
and you have pain passed down to you,
that you didn't deserve.
break the cycle of the toxicity that surrounds you
for the sake of your future.

if you've lost a loved one,

remember, i know it is hard,
and maybe they are physically gone, but there are
pieces of their soul that are embedded within you.
they are physically gone, but pieces of them will
remain to live on among you.
their lessons, their way of life, and their love still
exists. so they may not be here anymore,
but there is still pieces of them
that will remain to live on in this lifetime.

You're Everything You've Ever Needed

all that advice you give to others
it applies to you too,
don't be so hard on yourself.

You're Everything You've Ever Needed

i know you may not see it,
but be kind to yourself.
you advise everyone who needs it
but never to yourself.
you need to share if not the same,
more love into nurturing,
and caring for yourself as well.

You're Everything You've Ever Needed

the piece of them you still hold on to,
you need to let them go.
losing sleep over painfilled thoughts is not doing
you good, you need to let them go,
let yourself be free.

You're Everything You've Ever Needed

above all of those thoughts that keep you up,
above all of those thoughts that your bed seems to
be a magnate for, beneath it all.
i hope you find peace,
and i hope it lifts you out of this rut you're in.
i hope you heal,
i hope the best for you after all.

the right person, your person, would not leave you wondering if it is right.

You're Everything You've Ever Needed

your person, the right person,
would never do something to jeopardize your
relationship. the right person wouldn't leave you
wondering when they said they loved you last night
if it was true.
your person, the right person,
wouldn't leave you questioning your worth,
they wouldn't leave you wondering where you fit in
the puzzle, they would know
and so would you,
they would make sure of that.

you break your own heart everytime you romanticize them for someone they are not.

you create false realities of someone they will never be.

You're Everything You've Ever Needed

you have to stop romanticizing them.
you cannot keep making beautiful daydreams about them; when you do you are creating a version of them in your head that doesn't exist. you break your own heart everytime you think of that, because deep down you know they will never be the person you make them out to be.
ask yourself, why are you creating a version of them that does not exist, in hopes that they might be that person one day? you were perfect before them, you have been perfect all along, you are everything you've ever needed, you don't need that for yourself.

You're Everything You've Ever Needed

the sad truth is
if they wanted to be here, they
would

if they wanted to
they would be at your door, they wouldn't give up.
if they wanted to, they would.
you are everything you have ever needed all along
and one day, someone will love you and show you
that they want to; they will be at the door when you
want to leave to pull you back in,
they will make an effort.
don't hold onto someone who doesn't reciprocate the
same effort you put in,
you deserve more than that and
are worth so much more than that.

You're Everything You've Ever Needed

i'm staring at a blank paper,
i stumble upon what is meant to be spoken and trip
over what isn't. i'm staring at a blank piece of paper.
it has been 2 hours; time has stood still
since you've been gone, i'm still holding onto you,
i'm still holding onto the hope that i will wake up
from this dream and you will be here like you once
were.

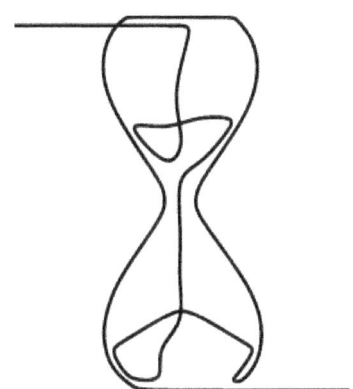

You're Everything You've Ever Needed

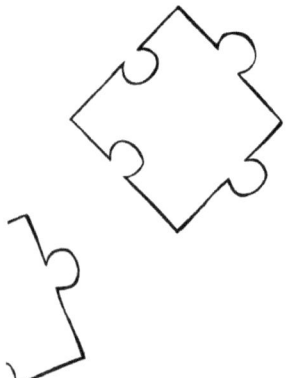
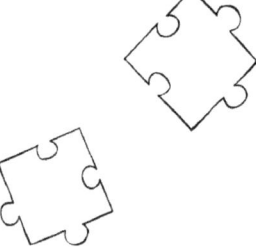

chapter three
healing

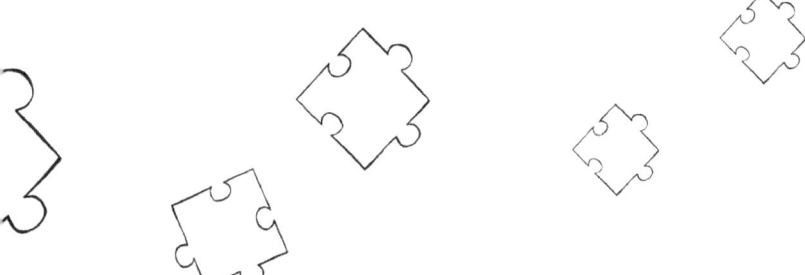

You're Everything You've Ever Needed

welcome every emotion you feel,
feel every moment of every laugh, and every cry.
allow yourself to be soaked within the pain,
and within the heartache.
don't let pain be fought off,
don't ignore your sadness,
don't let it be something to run from,
because what good was the heartache before then?

- *it is in your blood to feel*

healing isn't linear, it will leave you wondering if you are where you should be, and where you are supposed to be.

You're Everything You've Ever Needed

as you are healing, you will realize it is not linear but lonely. discovering that most people will leave is heartbreaking, but you never needed those people anyway. here you are doing it on your own, that is something to be proud of. you are deserving of love. do not let someone convince you of anything different. do not continue loving someone who isn't worthy of your love or effort. do not continue to break yourself by loving someone who can't reciprocate the same amount of effort you put in.

you deserve more than filtered words of false love.
you deserve unfiltered, passionate and gentle love.
one day, someone will show you that love is what you deserve instead of holding onto that hope alone.

discomfort, painful, and lonely
that is how i would describe healing if someone asked, but being healed is much more.
being healed is peaceful, it is freeing but once you are, do not let anyone get in-between that peace that was worked so hard for.

You're Everything You've Ever Needed

healing is messy, and it doesn't suddenly happen.
healing means feeling empowered one day, and then feeling lower than you may have ever felt.
healing doesn't suddenly happen; it is lonely, uncomfortable and scary. trusting others is hard, but trusting yourself and who you allow into your life without getting hurt may seem harder.
but i promise if you do the inner work,
the rest will follow, the rest will fall into place.

do not get in the way of yourself, put yourself first, love yourself, and care for yourself.

You're Everything You've Ever Needed

your presence fills a room of empty souls,
and your love filters the air.
your presence makes the room full,
it makes me feel full.

- *you are more powerful than you realize*

the addictive cycle of negative-thinking

you feel something is missing, you feel uncomfortable with the idea because if you can't think about all of what profoundly hurts you or has, you wonder if you will be anything. you wonder if you are anything, because those thoughts, these feelings have become a custom in your life.
you want to heal but wonder what you will be suitable for once you recover.

remember that healing isn't just about coming to terms and being at peace with whatever has caused you such pain or trauma. it is also about finding yourself and who you are as a person. so you may feel you won't be good for anything when you heal, *but you will discover everything you are best at once you heal.*

don't convince yourself that your dreams are out of reach, failure only exists if you stop trying.

You're Everything You've Ever Needed

what if the things we want most,
our dreams and desires take longer to come
because they are even more than what we worked
for, even more than what we dreamed for.
sometimes the things we want most,
are things we don't get immediately,
but knowing that makes it much more special.
so don't give up on that dream,
keep thriving, pushing, and doing what you love.
it is coming to you, so please don't give up.

change allows room for growth—change allows room for new opportunities—it isn't supposed to be comfortable.

You're Everything You've Ever Needed

reaching rock bottom is one of the most painful things we can endure, but it is best for us.
there is a purpose for things within this life, and there is a purpose for pain and human growth.
pain teaches us that scraping your knee on concrete is painful from an early age.
this is a controversial perspective, but i think pain teaches us how to grow. it teaches us what we accept and what we don't. it teaches us how much we can tolerate and what we won't. it is painful and lonely, but reaching rock bottom is like being reborn; you can let go of all the things you no longer need and can do better without.
reaching rock bottom is the best thing for us.

You're Everything You've Ever Needed

to heal from the person that broke you,
you must detach yourself from them,
from that initial attachment.
because if you do not, you will always
subconsciously search for them in every other
person you meet.

find a blank piece of paper and a pen
in that junk drawer.
ask yourself

what does your future look like?
what do you want your future to look like?
is what you're doing now aligned with the goals you have set?

are you happy?
if not, what would make that better?

peace will be the norm

love shouldn't be earned in a house you call home,
frustration shouldn't be screamed in raging anguish.
and home shouldn't be somewhere
to pack up all your trauma.

one day you will unlearn and detach from the
toxicity around you, one day your home will bring
you the peace you are searching for, and the peace
you need.

You're Everything You've Ever Needed

you make plans, only to cancel at the last minute.
you sleep your days away
and put headphones on to disconnect from every
thought, every memory, every feeling.
self-care doesn't mean isolating yourself
from the world. love, you have so much to look
forward to, and i know you don't see it now. but i
promise in one year, maybe five or ten, you will see
it and you will thank yourself for holding on and in
that time you will realize you should have been
kinder to yourself.

- *go easy on yourself, you're human*

you deserve to live, and you deserve to be your authentic self.

you deserve to do everything you desire in your life, you deserve to live, and be happy.

You're Everything You've Ever Needed

you are still here,
your heart still beats,
your brain is still running.
maybe it is running a thousand miles a minute, but
you are still here.
you deserve to be here,
you deserve to be here learning how to live and
learning what makes you happy.

You're Everything You've Ever Needed

you yearn to be loved the way you see it in movies, on social media, and you hope to be loved in ways you portray in your head. many people tell you it is unrealistic and love like that doesn't exist here, but i think it does. when the right person, your person, comes along, they will love you in all the ways you need and all the ways you want to be loved. someone will love you in ways maybe your past love didn't, but i promise the love that lives rent-free in your head exists, and you will be shown that one day it does, instead of holding onto that hope alone.

healing is realizing you have outgrown the person you once were, and accepting what cannot be undone but learning from it.

You're Everything You've Ever Needed

you are not the person you once were.
you are not the person they remember you as
and that is okay; let them be the version of you that
best fits them because deep down, you know that is
not you. you are not who you once were because
that part of you is a past that has been outgrown and
unlearned, so detach and dispute with the thought
that they may think you haven't.

You're Everything You've Ever Needed

deep down, you know you want more,
deep down, you know you deserve more.
but you don't want to leave and start over something
that hasn't quite finished, not wanting to start over
and not wanting to move on is not a reason to stay.
you deserve more, you deserve better,
you know you do.

You're Everything You've Ever Needed

you overlooked all those promises
they failed to keep.
you ignored all the rage boiling in their eyes and
gave them peace.
you ignored all the problems and toxicity,
and they looked for yours.
they picked out every flaw, because maybe then
they wouldn't feel so bad about their own.

reminder;
your feelings are valid

you do not need to search for validation to feel, you do not need someone to give you permission to feel. how we react to situations affects every person differently, so don't search for the validation that allows you to feel what you are feeling. it doesn't matter how big or small; give yourself permission to feel. you don't need to search for that from someone who doesn't feel the pain you have within you.

You're Everything You've Ever Needed

don't let them make you believe your basic needs are too much, and that asking for the bare minimum is too much.

- *simply, you are asking the wrong person*

You're Everything You've Ever Needed

your brain has grown inflamed since they've been gone; they have been a part of your life for quite some time, and now they are not here to hold, touch, hear, or feel you. your brain has now been inflamed because you are searching for them. you spend most days sleeping, but hiding from the pain only works when you are sleeping. once you awaken, it all comes flowing back, sometimes worse than before you fell asleep. it is emotionally exhausting, not to mention physically exhausting. let yourself feel the heartbreak. this feeling won't last forever, but feel it, and don't push it away while it is here. you think this way because you love and yearn for them, so hold onto this feeling.

You're Everything You've Ever Needed

stop staying in places you have outgrown and surrounding yourself with people you no longer feel connected to. it is not arrogant, and it is not selfish. simply, it means you are not wasting your life by living one that isn't your own. do not shrink yourself to please small-minded people.

your timing is on track

you are not behind because you are taking longer.
we will all get to the finish line in the end, so don't feel that you aren't as smart, as fast, or as intelligent because you are taking your time.
you cannot compare your journey to others,
they are not living your life.
you are the main character in your life, so don't feel your timing is off when you are just going at your own pace.

You're Everything You've Ever Needed

there is strength in doing what is best for you, in pursuing your own goals at your speed. there's no rule that your successes count less if you take longer to achieve them.

- *take your time*

you cannot help people that do not want to be helped, so do not lose yourself trying.

You're Everything You've Ever Needed

you cannot help them
if they cannot recognize their behaviors or actions
as hurtful or destructive.
you cannot change the toxicity that someone else
does not recognize. do not hurt yourself by trying to
help someone who doesn't want to be helped.

help the people who are willing
to be helped, help the people
who want to make change to
be better.

You're Everything You've Ever Needed

i know it's hard to watch someone you love hurt themselves from a toxic habit.
still, you cannot freely give all your time, effort and energy to those who don't make an effort to help themselves.
give that effort to yourself or to people who will appreciate it, and maybe one day,
they will reciprocate that effort to someone else who wants and needs that help too.

i am proud of you,

you should be proud too.
it is hard, but look how far you have come,
look how much you have grown.
i am proud of you for taking the steps and moving forward even when things have been hard, you did it, and you should be proud of yourself, too.

You're Everything You've Ever Needed

you worked so hard to get to where you are,
do not let small-minded people
belittle you or your success.
do not give them the power to send you back to
somewhere you fought so hard to get out of.

the right people will guide you in the right direction. the right people will bring you back to yourself, the right people will fight for you when things get hard,

and the right people will awaken that beauty that lies within you, not bring out the toxicity.
the right people will awaken the good that lies within.

You're Everything You've Ever Needed

when you learned how to walk, you fell,
when you learned how to run, you fell.
when you learned how to ride a bicycle, you fell.
and when you lost, you got up and continued to
keep going. just because things get complicated,
just because you hit bumps in the times of learning
doesn't mean you are failing,
it is simply a part of the process.

if you feel lost remember

you have a purpose,

you are just yet to find it.

You're Everything You've Ever Needed

you were put here for a purpose,
maybe you feel that you don't belong or don't have a purpose for being here, but you do.
you just haven't found it yet.
it will come, everyday you are putting it together piece-by-piece even when you don't realize it.
i promise it will come,
and you will figure it out soon enough.

grief is messy, dark, confusing, sad, and angry.
but that doesn't mean you are not healing,
there isn't a time frame for grieving.
some people grieve their whole life from a person, a childhood, or the loss of a loved one.
sometimes, people don't know what they are feeling is grief. but no matter how short or long, it is okay to feel how you feel. there isn't a time you aren't allowed to feel the feelings you are feeling, or have felt. sometimes, they will come back out of nowhere. it is beautiful in some ways, because you loved and yearned for something so much that it hurts. be kind to yourself, and ask for the help you may need, love the ones you care for, and hold them close.

there is goodness

in the pain that surrounds us.

believe in the goodness pain has, the perspective you change. the kindest people you meet aren't always born like that. some people are so kind and sweet that they are often taken for granted. they are the people who have fought and taken every lesson to better themselves to be who they are today. soft people are the ones who have walked through the mud, been dragged into the dark and chose not to let the darkness change them for the worse, but for the better.

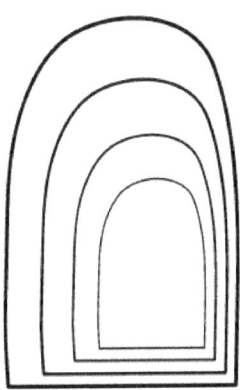

You're Everything You've Ever Needed

you scroll on social media and see someone you fantasize about, over-analyzing every inch of their body, from their hair to their skin, their curves or muscles, and wish you looked more like them. you overanalyze your body before you get in the shower and forget how lucky you are. you forget how beautiful or handsome people think you are as well. so don't wish you looked like someone else, everyone has their insecurities.
everyone is beautiful in their own way.

- *you're perfect the way you are*

You're Everything You've Ever Needed

there was something special about how they looked
deep into one another's their eyes,
they were full of love.
something was romanticizing about how they said
each other's names, and held each other when things
got hard. they showed everyone what love was
supposed to be, not what it wasn't.

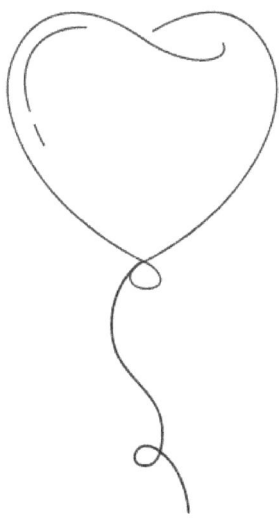

to love you have to let go of the fear of being hurt,

and to be loved you have to let your walls down to have the deepest and most honest connections.

You're Everything You've Ever Needed

a person who does not let themselves
feel the warmth of the love they are surrounded
with, will not love.
a person who will not let those walls down when
someone wants to give them the love they deserve,
the love they need,
they will spend the rest of their life feeling cold,
and walking around with armor on out of fear of
being hurt the way they once were.

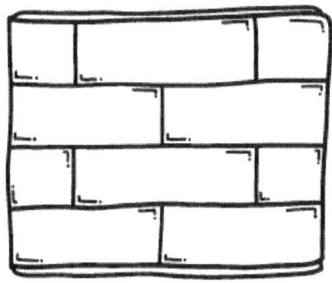

"they have potential"

a heart that is wrapped up for one person will leave you cold, empty, and numb. you will let them drag you through mud, through the darkest times and continue to let them. love through thick and thin, but do not bend your boundaries and values. you will leave yourself empty. you cannot love someone because they have potential, everyone has potential to be better and do better. but you cannot love someone for change, you cannot lay all your love down on a table and expect they will take it and give it all back to you. give all your love to yourself instead of the wrong person.

you will learn how to open up and love yourself the
way you love others, because you need that love
just as much as they do.
give all that love,
you so freely give to everyone to yourself.
put it back into your heart so it can pump the
remaining through your veins.
you will learn the power and value your love holds,
maybe then you will not give it
to people that do not deserve it.

let go, let yourself free from bad habits, toxic people and toxic behaviors.

You're Everything You've Ever Needed

let yourself outgrow certain people and toxic
behaviors that aren't good for you.
because then you can try new things,
learn new hobbies,
and meet new people who don't end up with bad
endings, or maybe no endings at all.
but perhaps opening yourself up to the good things
in life will make you believe you are worthy of
being happy and feeling loved as well.

they weren't meant to be in your life forever.

the people no longer in your life weren't meant to be here forever.
they were meant to be the ones who got away
because the right people stay,
and the people who see value,
fight for what they want.
they were simply just the ones
who were meant to get away.
they weren't meant to stay, because they would be here if they were.

to allow yourself to be free

don't think about if it is embarrassing,
people are too caught up in their own lives,
they do not care what the person in the mall was
wearing earlier that day when they go to sleep.
so don't lose sleep over what other people think
because when the sun sets at the end of the day,
does it matter?

you are allowed to be yourself, and you are allowed to take up space, stop letting yourself believe otherwise.

let them think wrong

don't exchange your peace to prove something to someone, don't destroy yourself trying to prove you are better, and don't let them have that power over you. you shouldn't need to prove to anyone that you are happy and at peace with yourself.

- *let people be wrong about you while you keep your peace*

You're Everything You've Ever Needed

healing requires
patience,
acceptance,
and perseverance.
healing does not happen overnight.
healing is painfully beautiful,
so don't feel you are behind or taking too long.

*take all the time you need
to return to yourself,*

*take all the time you need
to heal.*

You're Everything You've Ever Needed

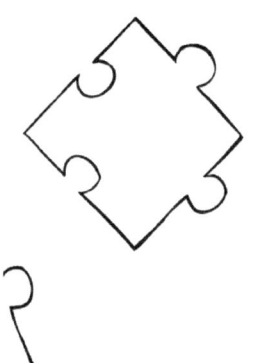

chapter four
growing

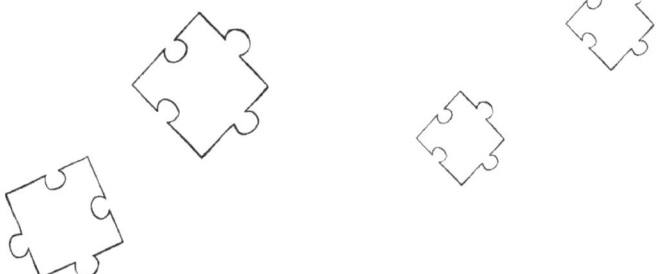

You're Everything You've Ever Needed

you are worth so much more than you think.

you will value peace
the closer you get to it

you will grow to be selective
of who you allow into your life,
you will appreciate your time,
your energy,
and you will value yourself.
you will learn along the way who is suitable for you
and who is good for your soul.
you will value yourself,
you will appreciate your peace,
but most importantly, your happiness.

You're Everything You've Ever Needed

*you will find the peace
you are fighting so hard to
find.*

the wrong people leave
so there is room for the right people.

You're Everything You've Ever Needed

there are reasons why things happen,
why people leave, and why people stay
when they know they shouldn't.
people come and go for the better,
people come and go so the right people have room
to come into your life, and the wrong people can go.
in time, you will realize you did not lose that
person, and may it hurt in the moment but
you were set free of someone or something that
wasn't a value to you.
you were set free of someone, of something less
than what you are deserving of.
you were set free of those people, so you have room
to allow those who are deserving, and who do value
you to come into your life and show you what love,
support and loyalty you have been searching for, the
love, support and loyalty you should have had all
along.

the painful truth is

the more chances you give them,
the more you stay when you know you should
leave, the less they respect you,
and the less you respect yourself.
you will be okay,
don't doubt yourself and how strong you are,
don't doubt your strength,
and how powerful you are.

the symbolic truth about toxic relationships

the self-destructive truth is,
when you continue to stay with someone
who isn't good for you, it is like walking along train
tracks, knowing a train is ahead.
it is like putting your hand on a burning hot stove
and holding it there.
you expect not to get hurt, and you keep doing it.
you keep forgiving them for their faults and
expecting them not to hurt the next time.
you've been here before, deep down, you know the
cycle will not end, why do you keep trying to
convince yourself otherwise?

- *if you take your hand off that stove, your hand will heal, and you will be okay*

when you feel it in your gut,
trust it, it's usually right.

You're Everything You've Ever Needed

if you are having a hard time separating anxiety and your intuition, do not ignore either of them.
feel them and acknowledge them, because the longer you ignore those feelings of unease.
the more it will consume you,
and the longer it will become painful.
sit with it, feel it, accept those feelings, and ask yourself where they may be coming from.
don't ignore the feelings that shouldn't be ignored and overlooked, the feelings that are screaming at you to be heard.

You're Everything You've Ever Needed

our bodies tell us what we need to know
before our minds discover.
when you feel unease,
when you think about that initial gut feeling,
that is your body's way of telling you they're not
suitable for you.
you shouldn't feel anxious with them, your body
will tell you when it's right
because you won't feel anything but
peace, happiness and clarity.
don't ignore your gut feeling,
don't ignore your body when it is trying to tell you
something just because you don't want to accept
what may be true.

You're Everything You've Ever Needed

you are right where you are meant to be

it may not seem or feel that way, but it is true.
things happen the way they are supposed to, when they are supposed to.
sometimes, they may not appear for the better, but one day, *you will realize the importance and purpose of timing.*

do not settle for love from the wrong person

the right person will be just as you imagined,
the right person will love you in all the ways you
need to be loved, and the right person will love you
in all the ways you've yearned all this time to be
loved.

the right person will love you in all the ways you need.

there is strength in your scars

their absence left a hole within you,
their absence left a void that grows
a void that craves to feel.
you were starved of the physical and emotional
connection you needed.
you were a stranger to love,
a stranger to feel.
a stranger to be heard,
and so you've had to carry it all alone.
one day, someone will come and give you that
security, love and connection you have been
searching for, but in the meantime,
as hard as it may be to take this time
to love yourself in all the ways you need to be
loved. discover all the things you've lost along the
way, and pick up all the pieces.
you have the strength within,
you just have to find it, and i promise you will.

You're Everything You've Ever Needed

the right person won't leave when times get hard

the right person will hold you tight,
you won't have to walk on eggshells around them,
they won't make you feel like you're too much.
the right person will love you,
all the good, all the bad
and all the pieces of you that you try to hide.

You're Everything You've Ever Needed

connection, security, and love
is how you cure that hatred that lives within.
that hatred you may carry does not fade away in
blocking out the world, it doesn't disappear when
you push everyone away.
the things you struggle with do not mean you must
or should carry them alone. allow yourself to reach
out to people, connect with people, and surround
yourself with positive people.

- *and watch how much strength you gain*

You're Everything You've Ever Needed

your pain,
your heartache,
doesn't make you unloveable.
you deserve to love yourself and be loved by those
around you.

you are the main character
in your life,
say no when you want
to say no.

You're Everything You've Ever Needed

you do not live by your boundaries,
by your values, or beliefs if when you feel
disrespected, you remain quiet.
when you say yes, when you want to say no
you go against everything you've worked so hard to
be. do not go against your beliefs or values,
do not lower yourself in worries about how another
person will think of you.
this is your life, you are the main character here.

the right person
is going to love you in all the
ways the wrong person couldn't.

You're Everything You've Ever Needed

the right person will love you
and one day, you're going to believe it too.
one day, you will see it, feel it, and hear it.
one day, you will live it.
the day you start to believe that love is what you are
deserving of, is the day you meet them,
is the day you will begin to feel it.

- *you're everything you've needed all along.*

self-love, self-respect, and happiness starts within,

it starts with being content with who you are, it starts with inner peace.

You're Everything You've Ever Needed

learn to be at peace with all the things
you don't talk about.
learn to love all the parts you isolate
from the rest of the world, and learn to love
all the parts you try to separate from yourself.

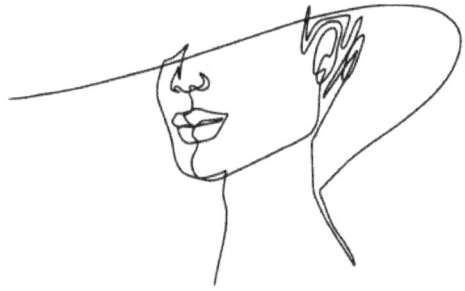

You're Everything You've Ever Needed

let them live their life,
so you can live yours

let them go,
let them live their life,
and let yourself let go of the hope they can or could
have been the person you needed.
let them go, let them live their life,
so you can live yours.

- *let go of the potential*

You're Everything You've Ever Needed

*you are doing so well
where you are*

i want you to close your eyes and remember a time
you used to pray to be where you are now.
i want you to take a minute and appreciate
how much you've grown,
i want you to understand that you are now
somewhere that you used to pray for,
and that is huge.

learn to appreciate your growth, and the progress you have made.

be grateful for the opportunities that surround you, and how much more there is to come.

You're Everything You've Ever Needed

hold onto the people,
you can laugh with,
the people you can cry with.
the people that you can sit in silence with
and just enjoy their company
without the exchange of a word.
hold those people close who genuinely listen to you.
the people who make you feel heard,
the people who make you feel seen make bonds.

- *the best kind of bonds*

You're Everything You've Ever Needed

the person they once knew
is not the person you are,
they do not know who you are now.
it is okay if they think you still are the person you
once were, the person you have outgrown.
if they have not been here to watch you grow and
change–you shouldn't worry about who they think
you are, because–the people who are important in
your life, know.

- *finding peace and comfort*

you cannot continue to break yourself for someone who doesn't want to make the change to be better.

you cannot continue to break yourself for someone who continuously walks all over you.

sometimes silence is better,
sometimes silence is louder than
you could ever scream.
silent cut-offs sometimes are the answer because
how many times do you tell a person that they are
hurting you, that what they are doing is not okay
before you lose yourself in the hope that they will
one day hear you.

- *sometimes it is the only answer*

you are forever changing,
forever growing,
and evolving,
it is okay to outgrow people.

you can miss someone, and you can love someone but hate the person they have become.
it is okay to miss who a person was–to which they have outgrown–to grieve that person because a part of them is gone that you loved, is beautiful in its own way.

- *forever changing*

You're Everything You've Ever Needed

you are brave to give such a fragile part of you to someone and trust them with it.
but if they have broken that trust,
do not close yourself off out of fear of having your heart broken; not everyone is out to hurt.
maybe they didn't mean to hurt you, but somehow, some way, they still did.
not everyone will.
so fall in love one more time,
what was the last heartbreak worth
if you can't give yourself the chance to love and be loved again?

- *learning lessons*

You're Everything You've Ever Needed

i know you can still draw their face like the map of
a too-familiar road, i know you could still pick them
out in a crowd of people,
but remember that so many other people love you,
and this isn't the end of the world, it will get better
soon enough.

- *give yourself time to heal*
  and you will see it too

You're Everything You've Ever Needed

if you've lost a loved one

i don't know why forever wasn't a part of the story; i don't understand why some people leave this lifetime before we're ready to let go, but hold onto those pieces of them that made a home within, hold on the glimpses of memories,
hold on to the love.

knowing you loved someone so much that
it's painful, is beautiful. but grieving a loss is not about moving on, because i don't think you can ever truly move on from someone you love that much. coming to terms with that unfortunately things happen the way they are supposed to, when they are supposed to even when we don't want them to.

- *let it give you the comfort and clarity you are searching for*

You're Everything You've Ever Needed

you should not be screaming to be heard,
to be respected,
to be loved,
or to feel safe.
love shouldn't hurt,
you deserve more than a so-called love like this.

You're Everything You've Ever Needed

you're doing so much better than you realize

you're still here through all of the heartache,
all of the loss and grief.
you're still here,
you are healing, and reclaiming all of the pieces of
you that were lost along the way.
you're still here, and you're healing
more than you realize.

You're Everything You've Ever Needed

you're not alone

it may feel like it at times, but you're not.
there are people out there struggling, and going through the same thing you are, so don't feel that you are alone. you are worth so much more than the pain, so much more than what you are feeling.
there is light at the end of this; you're not alone because i'm here with you too.

You're Everything You've Ever Needed

if they weren't suitable for you,
if they weren't made for you, that is okay.
because that means you must have been made for someone else, too.

healing will change you

you will cut off those that are not providing you
with the peace you fought so hard to reach.
healing will cost you comfort,
and stability for sometime.
because it is change, and change is different.
there are a lot of different feelings and thoughts that
will come your way in this time, and that is normal.
healing will change you,
healing will bring you peace,
and acceptance,
but most of all it will bring you happiness.

healing will lead you back to pieces of you; the good pieces.

You're Everything You've Ever Needed

you will grow and learn,
you will find the strength within to heal from
whatever may come your way.
you will love different,
you will care for others different,
you won't waste your time trying to prove a point
that will never be understood.
you will be at peace,
you will be a home to yourself,
and you won't let yourself be treated anything less
than what you are worth.

You're Everything You've Ever Needed

let go of people that don't provide you peace.

You're Everything You've Ever Needed

let go of the toxic people,
put yourself first.
leave the things behind that don't make you happy.
you won't regret being the person deep down,
you know you need to be to take care of yourself.

You're Everything You've Ever Needed

even sometimes when the world feels like it just came crashing down, it is a breakthrough,
it is freedom.
it was the peace you needed,
sometimes the things we ask for often come in the most unexpected ways–the things we ask for may require us to leave behind other things in exchange–because it wasn't doing us good.
sometimes, the things we lose are for clarity,
are for peace, and the freedom you know deep down you need, and that you deserve.

being happy,
and feeling contentment

<u>was never about the things</u>
<u>that bring you</u>
<u>temporary happiness.</u>

You're Everything You've Ever Needed

truly being happy
is being comfortable with yourself.
it is coming terms and accepting that the things that
happen in your life aren't always your fault,
that you can move forward, leaving what is meant
to be in the past.
truly being happy doesn't mean you won't have
sudden sadness and anger because that is all a part
of reaching the peace you deserve and are fighting
for.

You're Everything You've Ever Needed

you are inspiring

throughout everything you have endured,
you are here pushing through.
you are still achieving all the good things,
even if you don't recognize those achievements.
if no one has told you,
i'm here to remind you i am proud of you,
and who you are.

perspective of life

prioritize yourself,
heal yourself,
embody love and watch how your life changes.
your positive thoughts and assumptions are a reflection of your mind.
external changes begin with internal change first,
be your unapologetic, authentic self.
this is your reality, this is your life.

reminder:

love shouldn't leave you feeling uncertain and hungry.

love should leave you feeling whole, and full.

You're Everything You've Ever Needed

their opinions do not matter,
they hold no significance in your life,
people are too caught up in their own lives
to worry about yours.

- *let yourself be free*

the law of attraction

a lot of us stay in relationships that we are not
happy in because of the time, effort and love that
has been put into the relationship.
you have nothing to lose, well you only have to lose
the time you were unhappy, but you do not have to
relearn someone else.
you can take the time to do the things you love
you can learn about yourself,
what you love and what you don't.

- *the right people will come to you*

the right people will come to you, and everything else will fall into place.

you hold all the power in who you allow in your life.

what you allow and don't allow, starts within and ends there too.

<u>*if it hurts,*</u>

<u>*it's not right for you.*</u>

read that again.

nothing is wrong with you,
do not keep doing something that doesn't feel good.
just because it works for them, does not mean it will work for you. do not keep pushing yourself to make something work that isn't meant to.

- *be yourself*

*let yourself feel
your feelings, you're human.*

You're Everything You've Ever Needed

don't drink it away,
don't smoke it away,
don't sleep it away
and don't try to fill it with meaningless sex.

feel it, and feel it more.
sitting with it, acknowledging it, and feeling it,
sometimes, is the only way to heal.

You're Everything You've Ever Needed

it is not love that has hurt you, it is the lack of it.

You're Everything You've Ever Needed

i'm sorry that love has been a word that reminds you of everything wrong that has occurred because of the lack of it.

you have placed a heart-shaped box under your bed, and it has grown to be covered in dust and hate.

i'm sorry you've spent your time building a wall that surrounds you so no one can come close enough to see that love is what you are hiding from, love is what you think you are hiding from. you are hiding from the lack of love you were shown, the lack of love has hurt you.

you cannot allow yourself to be loved in all the right ways, if you have a wall with a sign that says "no trespassing", you cannot let yourself give the love you need either.

You're Everything You've Ever Needed

why do you need them to validate
how they make you feel?
as if it isn't real unless they tell you it is,
why do you need them to validate
the pain they caused you,
to give you permission to feel it?
you need to let them go,
if they decided to put your relationship or friendship
at risk, they did not value you or the relationship.
you deserve more than that,
you deserve to surround yourself with people who
appreciate, love, and respect you
let the others go.

if you want to detach yourself from that person,

you need to detach yourself from what you need from them.

You're Everything You've Ever Needed

you will grow,
and fall over and over again. you are going to have wins in this lifetime,
and you are going to have losses.
you will continue to have them, because that is life.
don't be scared to try something new out of fear of failure. loss is how you learn, loss is how you grow.
you have to find the light in the darkness surrounding you.

the nature of the universe will tell you, if they are not meant for you.

You're Everything You've Ever Needed

you know when something is not right,
you know when someone is not suitable for you.
you cannot make excuses for them
because you do not want to start over
and accept what may be the truth.

You're Everything You've Ever Needed

a cycle of reliving what hurt you,
and replaying it in your head
does not mean you aren't healing.
you find comfort in the pain.
safety, and security, too maybe.

reliving your trauma
does not mean you aren't healing,
it just means you are working with all
that you've ever known of.
a big part of healing is sitting with those emotions
and feelings.

this varies from one person to the next,
so don't compare your version of healing to the next
person, because we all heal differently.

*you are not your trauma,
you are not the bad things
that have happened to you.*

You're Everything You've Ever Needed

you are not a damaged piece
or an unfixable good, because you have had to
experience traumatic things.
you are not your trauma and it may hurt
but you are so much more than
the pain you have endured.

You're Everything You've Ever Needed

some people will never see things
from a different perspective, or even try.
do not drain yourself trying to prove something to
someone who will never see it from a different
perspective.
love them, hate them, or forgive them.
but don't hurt yourself by trying to prove something
to someone who will never see it from a different
point of view, you will end up exhausted and tired.

some people don't want to see things in a different light, and that is okay.

You're Everything You've Ever Needed

learn what you need for yourself,
what you want,
and what leaves you feeling fulfilled,
so you don't waste your time on what doesn't.

You're Everything You've Ever Needed

*you are everything
you have ever needed,
all along.*

You're Everything You've Ever Needed

self-love is a lonely journey,
and most people will mistake it for being selfish but
sometimes you have to be.

at one point in your life,
you have to think for yourself,
you have to do what you need,
you have to be the person you need,
not just the person they want you to be for them.

You're Everything You've Ever Needed

happiness was never about the things that make you
temporarily happy.

that new bag you just bought,
that person you hooked up with at a party,
or even hanging out with people so you never have
to sit alone with your own thoughts.

- *those rushes of dopamine are short term,*
and will not last forever

grow to enjoy your own company, and learn to be comfortable being uncomfortable.

You're Everything You've Ever Needed

unpack all your feelings, all your traumas that you
have pushed under the rug. sit with them, feel them,
and slowly do the inner work.
healing is uncomfortable so learn
to be comfortable with being uncomfortable.
your happiness, that contentment
and that peace you are searching for
is not far from you.
it is not about finding a person to distract you or
"heal" you. it is not about *being loved*
or allowing yourself *to love.*
it is about acknowledging that this is your life and
you make the change to be the best person you can
be for yourself. you write the narrative and
create your reality.

you are everything you've ever needed all along
throughout this journey and everything you will
ever need to be the person deep down you know you
need to be for yourself.

it was about finding yourself,
and realizing,

you are everything you need to
to be the person you want to
be, and the person you need to
be.

www.ingramcontent.com/pod-product-compliance
Lightning Source LLC
Chambersburg PA
CBHW072153070526
44585CB00015B/1124